Tell Your Truth
becoming vulnerable enough to change

Brandon J. Addison

Tell Your Truth

Brandon J. Addison

ISBN: 979-8-9867501-0-1

Copyright © 2022 Brandon J Addison

All rights reserved under International Copyright Law. Contents and/or cover may not be reproduced in whole or in part in any form without the express written consent of the publisher.

All scripture quotations, unless otherwise indicated, are taken from the King James Version of the Holy Bible. Scripture quotations marked "NKJV" are taken from the New King James Version®. Copyright © 1982 by Thomas Nelson. Used by permission. All rights reserved. Scripture quotations marked "NIV" are taken from the Holy Bible, New International Version®. Copyright © 1973, 1978, 1984 by International Bible Society. Used by permission of Zondervan Publishing House. All rights reserved. Scripture quotations marked "ESV" are taken from The Holy Bible, English Standard Version®. Copyright © 2001 by Crossway, a publishing ministry of Good News Publishers. All rights reserved. Used by permission.

Brandon J. Addison

Table of Contents

Table of Contents i

Dedication 1

Acknowledgments 1

Introduction 1

What A Promise From God Looks Like 5

    A Test of Faith 5

    Relationships Build Faith 9

    His Grace Is Enough 12

    Abraham, Isaac, and the Cross of Jesus 13

    Certitude, The Hope We Have in Him 15

    I Almost Committed a Felony 16

God Is Greater Than Your Past Mistakes 19

    Why We Have Religious Differences 30

    Illegitimate Child 34

The Blessings of God 41

Battlefield Of The Mind 60

No Resurrection Without Death 79

   Promise - Salvation 79

   What Happens After Death 88

   What Christ Endured For Us 97

   The Truth About The Resurrection 100

Straightway 103

About The Author 116

Brandon J. Addison

Dedication

This book is dedicated to my daughter Keilani Rose. The same three years I spent writing and publishing this book, I spent fighting for her.

Acknowledgments

My mom and dad Linda and Vernon Addison, my brothers and sister. My pastor Dr. Walter Malone Jr. my mentor Dr. Otis K. Bush, My scribe A. Williams. Charles Harrison who planted the first financial seed to publish this book. Stephon Camp, Ashley Davis, and the whole Kingdom Advancement Cathedral of Worship church family for allowing me to be the Pastor God called me to be not the Pastor, they wanted me to be. The Entire Hopeboyz nation, All sponsors of the Hopeboyz Podcast and all my followers and subscribers.

Introduction

I am a fourth-generation minister, a third-generation pastor, and a second-generation founding pastor. I am honored to be a part of such an anointed heritage. My grandfather, Joseph Zachariah Windley, always told me that it is impossible to claim what you believe is right, and to claim what someone else believes is wrong if you do not know what they believe.

The Word of God is a complex truth. It takes serious prayer, study, and discernment to rightly divide God's Word. The Bible tells us in 2nd Timothy 2:15, *"Study to shew thyself approved unto God, a workman that needeth not to be ashamed, rightly dividing the word of truth."* So, when studying the Word of God, the best way to get the full meaning of a passage is to read at least five verses prior and five verses after. This is called "digging for meat."

I have colleagues in the ministry who proclaim the Word of God from Genesis to Revelation to make sure they are teaching the whole Bible. I have other friends who pick and pluck through the Word to manipulate it to say what they want it to say. However, I am one of many who allows the Holy Spirit to guide us to what is most imperative to the spiritual growth and kingdom advancement of the flock. I believe the cannon is closed, and Jesus Christ is the highest revelation of God known to man.

Telling one's own truth can be such an uncomfortable topic that many church leaders choose to avoid it. However, I choose to be transparent as God leads, knowing that the magnanimous God I serve is powerful and all-knowing. He is the Alpha and the Omega. He is my Healer. He is my Provider. His name is I AM. We are made in the likeness of God. Even if He does not do anything else for me, I will still worship Him because of who He is. If He says to be transparent and tell my truth, then I will do it.

As we move forward, I urge you to pay close attention to the honesty I share about my life. Also, pay close attention to the convictions God brings to light within your own life. You will see three different truths. You will see truths that I speak about my life, truths God convicts you of in your life, and truths about the church as a whole. When I say the church as a whole, I mean the greater body of the Christian community.

I prophesy that as you work your way through this book, you will experience a spiritual rebirth. I prophesy a spiritual rebirth in you. I prophesy that a fire is reignited in you at the altar with prayer and praise. I prophesy that our lives are saturated and continually soaked in the smoke of the Holy Spirit. I prophesy that the Glory of God will be so strong in our lives that it will be likened to the days in 1 Kings 8:11, where the priests could not perform their service because the Glory of the Lord filled the temple.

What A Promise From God Looks Like

A Test of Faith

Then Moses said to God, "Indeed, when I come to the children of Israel and say to them, 'The God of your fathers has sent me to you,' and they say to me, 'What is His name?' what shall I say to them?" And God said to Moses, "I AM WHO I AM." "Thus you shall say to the children of Israel, 'I AM has sent me to you.'"—Exodus 3:13-15 NKJV

God said His name is I AM. We are made in the likeness of Him. We are designed to look like Him. We have minds to understand and think like Him. We have mouths to speak like Him. We have the potential to take part in an awesome future in His very family. You are made in the likeness of God to live as who you truly are. You must believe in, trust in, listen to God and obey Him. Abraham was a man who did just that.

Abraham is seen as the "Father of the Faith" for Christians, and he is honored for his obedience. He is an example of how to trust God, especially when it comes to the hard stuff. We can learn a lot from Abraham.

"The Lord had said to Abram, "Go from your country, your people and your father's household to the land I will show you. "I will make you into a great nation, and I will bless you; I will make your name great, and you will be a blessing. I will bless those who bless you, and whoever curses you I will curse; and all peoples on earth will be blessed through you." So, Abram went, as the Lord had told him; and Lot went with him. Abram was seventy-five years old when he set out from Harran." Genesis 12:1-4

So, God told him to leave his native land of Ur and journey to a land and a people that he did not know. He stepped out in faith, and he and his household began a journey to an unknown destination, never to return to his homeland again. He was 75 years old.

Today, most people would question God on that one, saying, "Lord, You know I am retired now. I like it here. I'm too old to be moving around now, especially going to some place I don't know." But Abram trusted God and went out, not knowing where he was going (Hebrews 11:8). He arrived in the land God said He would give to his descendants. As Abram obeyed and grew in faith, God continued to reveal to him the blessings he and his descendants would receive (Genesis 13:2; Genesis 14:17, Genesis 15:4-6, Genesis 18).

God prophesied to Abram and to his wife, Sarai, who was barren. He promised that they would have a child, and that child would give Abram more descendants than the stars in the sky. Then God promised Abram that he and

Sarai would be father and mother of many nations. (Genesis 17:1-8; 15-16) Sarah laughed and thought to herself that Abram is too old, and I have been barren my entire life. (Genesis 18:12)

Has God ever done something so miraculous in your life that all you could do was laugh and say God has done it again? There is no other way you could explain what happened. You know it was God. Sarai laughed, but God did just as He said He would, and that prophecy is still being fulfilled today.

We also see in Genesis chapter 17 that God changed Abram's name to Abraham, which means "The Father of Many Nations," and Sarai's name to Sarah. Abraham is the father of three of the five major monotheistic religions of the world: Judaism, Islam, and Christianity. Because of that, I consider all Jews, Muslims, and Christians as brothers. The difference is, Christians accept Jesus Christ as their Lord and Savior, while Jews and Muslims see Him only as a prophet.

When Abraham turned 100 years old, God blessed him with the child He had promised. Through every valley, through every struggle, through his disbelief, and even through his fleshly desires, God's promise continues to prevail.

Relationships Build Faith

Genesis 22 opens with God testing Abraham.

"1 Now it came to pass after these things that God tested Abraham, and said to him, "Abraham!" And he said, "Here I am." 2 Then He said, "Take now your son, your only son Isaac, whom you love, and go to the land of Moriah, and offer him there as a burnt offering on one of the mountains of which I shall tell you."

Isaac was Abraham's second son. The love Abraham had for Isaac was perhaps no greater than the love he had for Ishmael, but Abraham's relationship with God was made known through his son Isaac, and the promise made to him was through his son Isaac. It is interesting to watch the obedience of Abraham to God's instructions. God told him to go sacrifice his son, and early the next morning he left for Mount Moriah.

One thing I know for sure is that pillow talk is real. I would have loved to be a fly on the wall that night. I would have loved to see Abraham walking into the tent and saying, "Sarah, tomorrow I must leave and take our son to Mount Mariah and sacrifice him to the Lord. Yes, the Lord told me to sacrifice the son I love, the one I waited 100 years for." Knowing how a mother gets about her child who is in trouble, I can only imagine Sarah's response to her husband wanting to sacrifice the son she'd waited 100 years for. The son that made her laugh at God. I imagine her response was not a good one, or maybe she too had grown in her faith and relationship with God as Abraham had. The scripture doesn't say.

"Early the next morning, Abraham got up and loaded his donkey. He took with him two of his servants and his son Isaac. When he had cut enough wood for the burnt offering, he set out for the place God had told him about. On the third day, Abraham looked up and saw the place in the distance. He said to his servants, "Stay here with the donkey while the boy and I go over there. We will worship, and then we will come back to you.""—Genesis 22:3-4

When you have certitude in God, you will trust God and go with confidence because you know Him and trust that He will do what He has promised. Because Abraham had that certitude, he realized that his son was key to the promise God made to him. He knew God would produce more descendants than the stars in the sky. There is no way God would allow Isaac to die. So, Abraham told his servants to wait there, and they would both be back.

His Grace Is Enough

Like most young men, Isaac was curious. He saw the fire, the wood, and the knife they carried, but no lamb. He asked his father, *"Where is the lamb for a burnt offering?"* (Genesis 22:7 NKJV) Abraham answered, *"My son, God will provide,"* (Genesis 22:8 NKJV).

You are an example to your children of what faith looks like. If you do not have what is called "certitude" you cannot expect your child to ever have faith. Isaac's obedient faith to submit to his own sacrifice is just as incredible as his father's. As a parent, I imagine even with his certitude, Abraham must have felt much anxiety and pain as he and his son walked up that mountain. I can almost see him moving slowly, taking his time waiting on God to move. I imagine he was inwardly calling out to God, "Anytime now, God. You can move in this situation any time."

In old Jewish tradition, it was customary for people to slit their sacrifice on the neck and bless it, and then light the wood on fire underneath the sacrifice. Abraham bound his son to the altar and was prepared to slice his son's neck, believing that God would work a miracle and honor His promise. God stopped Abraham and said, *"Do not lay your hand on the lad, or do anything to him; for now, I know that you fear God, since you have not withheld your son, your only son, from Me"* (Genesis 22:12 NIV). When God stretched out His hand that day to rescue Isaac, He did so at the very last second. His timing is similar in our lives. He may not come when you want Him, but He will be right on time.

Abraham, Isaac, and the Cross of Jesus

The foresight of God is incredible! The entire Bible points to Jesus. This is especially true of Abraham and Isaac's story. In this story, Isaac represents Jesus, and Abraham represents God. This open exchange in Genesis 22 points to the cross of Christ. Notice that both Isaac and Jesus are long-awaited "beloved sons" born in miraculous circumstances. Isaac carried the wood for his sacrifice on his back. Jesus carried the cross of His sacrifice on His back. Both Isaac and Jesus were led by their father to be sacrificed, and the sons followed obediently toward his own death.

God provides a lamb for the sacrifice in Isaac's place. Jesus was the sacrificial Lamb, slain from the foundation of the world as the sacrifice once and for all for the sins of the world. Abraham and Isaac traveled three days to Mount Moriah and Isaac was bound to the altar. Jesus was bound to the cross. He died and was buried for three days, then He rose with all power in His hands so that you and I could be forgiven.

Abraham and Isaac's actions that day provided a model of obedience that is surpassed only by the act of Jesus at the cross of Calvary. We have grace through the Blood of Jesus Christ, but during Abraham and Isaac's lifetimes, Christ had not yet died on the cross.

Certitude, The Hope We Have in Him

You must have certitude in God. Certitude means having the utmost confidence in something; it is absolute certainty or conviction that something is the case. Certitude is operating on meat of the Word, not milk. Certitude says that you do not have to see it to believe it. The belief that the next time you take a breath, you will be able to breathe is an example of certitude. The things that you do without ever thinking about them, is an example of certitude.

Certitude says that God is your fortress and your strength. Certitude says God is your Healer, Jehovah Rapha. Certitude says God is your Deliverer, God is your Banner (Jehovah Nissi). Certitude says that God is your Peace (Jehovah Shalom). Certitude says that God is your Righteousness (Jehovah Tsidkenu). Certitude says that God is your Shepherd (Jehovah Rohi). Certitude says God is my Provider (Jehovah Jireh). Certitude says God is your Abiding Presence (Jehovah Shammah).

Certitude says God is your Rock in a weary land. Certitude says God is your Light in the darkness—even though I walk through the valley of the shadow of death, I will fear no evil, for You are with me. Certitude means I have the confidence that when God speaks and makes a promise, He means it, and it is guaranteed to come to fruition.

I Almost Committed a Felony

Just like with Abraham, God tested me and put me in an uncomfortable situation. Our church had been on a spiritual high. We moved quickly into our facility and the next thing we knew we had a food trailer for God's Grill to feed the homeless. We were floating on cloud nine because of what we were able to accomplish with feeding the homeless. Everyone who was involved was blessed at a level that I do not think they even realized was coming.

Often, blessings do not come by happenstance or circumstance but purely by vision, faith, prayer, and fasting. I recall the day when I almost committed a felony. Yes, I could have been prosecuted and sent to jail. But God! I was experiencing a similar test as Abraham. Believing and knowing what God had told me, I pushed and pushed forward, remembering the words of my co-pastor. I thank God for Co-Pastor Thornton. Mentally, he kept me together and organized. His words, "just keep doing what you're doing," kept coming to me.

My mentors and advisors expressed concern for me. They asked me what I would do if I ended up in jail. My response was that if I end up in jail, I will be preaching from jail, but I have got my eye on the prize, and I know God will provide and take care of me. I said that I would be like Paul, and write and teach from a jail cell, but nothing will stop me from completing what God has called me to do.

I got in my car and made my way to Evansville. I was meeting with a guy named Kevin. I handed Kevin a $6,000 check with $2,000 to back it up. I hooked up the God's Grill trailer and pulled off. I prayed, "Lord, it's all in your hands. You told me to feed the homeless at a capacity I have never seen before. That was a promise from God that the Kingdom Advancement Cathedral of Worship would be a leader in the feeding and salvation of the homeless in Louisville, Kentucky.

Before the check could be cashed, God placed a ram in the bush. A young brother with no membership in the church told me that he finally got on disability and was paid all of his back pay. He placed the remaining balance in my hand. When you walk by faith and have certitude in God, He will always operate in grace and place a ram in your bush.

God Is Greater Than Your Past Mistakes

You know, sometimes when God speaks to us or prophesies to us, it doesn't happen right away. Sometimes it does, but most times it doesn't. This was the case with Abraham and Sarah. Years went by and the child God promised them, had not yet come. Abraham and Sarah began to question God, thinking that maybe they didn't hear God correctly. Maybe they misunderstood how it was supposed to happen. They hatched a plan to bring the prophecy to fruition.

Sarah decided to create a child through her Egyptian servant, Hagar, who was a gift from Pharaoh (Genesis 12:10-20). Sarah reasoned that when the child was born, it would belong to her, and they would finally have the child God promised. So, Sarah told her husband Abraham to lie with the servant woman Hagar. Abraham agreed and Hagar conceived and bore a son whom they called Ishmael.

After Hagar conceived, she took advantage of her new position and began to look down on Sarah and dishonor her. Likewise, Sarah mistreated Hagar—so much so that Hagar fled into the wilderness. She must have been afraid and feeling pretty hopeless out there in the middle of nowhere. But God did not abandon Hagar. He offered Hagar and her unborn child hope.

"The angel of the Lord found Hagar near a spring in the desert; it was the spring that is beside the road to Shur. And he said, Hagar, slave of Sarai, where have you come from, and where are you going?" "I'm running away from my mistress Sarai," she answered. Then the angel of the Lord told her, "Go back to your mistress and submit to her." The angel added, "I will in-

crease your descendants so much that they will be too numerous to count." The angel of the Lord also said to her: "You are now pregnant, and you will give birth to a son. You shall name him Ishmael, for the Lord has heard of your misery. He will be a wild donkey of a man; his hand will be against everyone and everyone's hand against him, and he will live in hostility toward all his brothers."—Genesis 16: 7-12 NIV

Notice that God's promise to Hagar is very similar to His promise to Abram. With that, Hagar entered a relationship with God that changed her identity and her perspective. She was no longer just a slave, but an heir to God's promise. She responded by saying to the Lord, "You are the God who sees me," for she said, "I have now seen the One who sees me." (Genesis 16:13) Hagar returned to Abram and Sarai's household. This was the beginning of what today we call baby mama drama.

At the appointed time, Hagar gave birth to a son and named him Ishmael. But for Sarah, it was not like having a child of her very own as she had imagined. God said to Abraham that although I will bless your son Ishmael, he is not the promised child. Genesis chapter 21 opens with Sarah finally becoming pregnant and giving birth to her one and only child. After 25 years of waiting, and fourteen years after Ishmael was born, Sarah gave birth to a son and named him Isaac, which in Hebrew means "laughter." This name was quite fitting because even after Sarah mocked God, He still provided. Abraham was ecstatic to have received a son at the age of 100. Sarah proclaimed there was no way anyone could not laugh at this situation. God had given her a child at 90 years of age.

Isaac grew and was weaned according to Jewish custom. The Hebrew word for weaned means "to become a person." So, when the Bible says that a male child has been weaned, it is not referring to being weaned from breast milk, but rather it means "becoming of a man." This is the time when a mother sends her son off to be with his father to learn how to become a man. No woman can truly teach her son to be a man. She can raise him to become an adult, but how to be a man, he must learn that from a man; whether that man is the boy's actual father or just a father-figure in his life, but it still takes a man to teach a boy to be a man.

In the Jewish custom, the firstborn son is taken very seriously. This is similar to our custom today, where often the firstborn son is named after his father. On the day Isaac was weaned, Abraham held a great feast (Genesis 21:8). The Jewish people still throw parties when their children become adults, called a bar mitzvah or bat mitzvah.

After fourteen years, Abraham's polygamous style family dynamics had reached a breaking point. Sarah saw fourteen-year-old

Ishmael mocking her newly weaned Isaac. She thought that since Isaac was not the first-born son, there was no way Isaac would still receive the blessing that God had bestowed upon this family. This mocking took the baby mama drama to another level. Sarah complained to Abraham, saying, *"Get rid of that slave woman and her son. He is not going to share the inheritance with my son, Isaac. I won't have it!" (Genesis 21:10 NLT).*

Sarah's demand troubled Abraham. He didn't know what to do about the issue between his wife and his baby mama—after all, Ishmael was also his son. God spoke to him and told him not to feel badly about the boy and his mother.

"But God said to him, "Do not be so distressed about the boy and your slave woman. Listen to whatever Sarah tells you, because it is through Isaac that your offspring will be reckoned. I will make the son of the slave into a nation

also, because he is your offspring."
—*Genesis 21:12-13 NIV*

After hearing from the Lord, Abraham packed up some food and water and sent Hagar and Ishmael on their way. I find it ironic that Abraham gave the three visitors (Genesis 18) more than he gave to his own flesh and blood and the slave woman when she left. Today, many times, a parent will give as little child support as possible for his or her child.

Have you ever encountered someone that you wanted to call...anything but a child of God? Maybe you've faced some baby mama drama? Oh, she's cool when she is 'acting right.' But what about on pick up and drop off day and she's looking at you sideways as she walks out of the house with a little too few clothes on. Maybe she left her hand on your husband's arm just a little bit too long. She touched your husband one too many times. It is obvious that she is trying to get her man back and you wanted to go off on her and call her anything but a child of God. Or maybe it was you who was called everything but a child of God?

Oh, you don't have that kind of drama in your life. Well, let me see if I go up another street and land on your block. Remember back in 2016, when Donald J. Trump was elected to office and our counterparts thought it was okay to publicly show their racism and commit racist acts? They figured, since our president has no filter, neither should we. We made it to 2020, and we thought we were almost done with the blatant racism. Then, unfortunately, deaths of African Americans began to occur more often across our nation, and we decided that we were outraged enough to protest. Friends, coworkers, neighbors, and store clerks alike all responded in a way that shocked us.

The little faith we had in other races was torn down. It seemed like the country was publicly humiliating black and brown people.

They called us the "N" word in front of the world, as if they were saying, "What now? How did that affect you? Did you become enraged?" That feeling of rage can take hold of you, and you begin to understand where Sarah is coming from. But understand this much, you did it to yourself.

Americans and many other societies as a whole do not respect the sanctity of marriage enough not to have baby mamas once, twice, or even more times. Too many minorities do not appreciate the right to vote enough, so we don't educate ourselves and vote in every election. Presidents are elected by the electoral college, not by the popular vote. So, if you wait to vote every four years, you are too late.

Hagar and Sarah started a bunch of baby mama drama, but baby daddies are just as bad. The reality was that Abraham could not keep it in his pants. He and his wife Sarah's inability to have certitude in God is the primary reason this entire situation took place.

When Sarah presented her maidservant to Abraham, his response should have been, "No, God will provide." Instead, he agreed. One of the main reasons I believe the terms "baby mama" and "baby daddy" are so degrading is because that person is your child's parent.

After his wife Sarah died, Abraham took another concubine a.k.a Baby mama, named Keturah. She bore him six sons, Zimran, Jokshan, Medan, Midian, Ishbak, and Shuah. According to Genesis 25:6, Abraham gave them gifts and sent them off to a land in the east, away from Isaac. This is after he was already past 100 years old and now that he was blessed with the ability to have kids, instead of stopping with the promised child, he got married and had six more sons. He couldn't keep it in his pants.

My point is the mighty men and women in the Word of God and in the world today are human. They messed up just like the rest of us and made some of the same mistakes we make today. No one is perfect, but sometimes you have to step up to the plate, examine yourself, and realize that you're wrong sometimes too. Abraham, Sarah, and Hagar's relationship is an example of why I believe polygamy is wrong. Scripture tells us that adultery is wrong. However, as a society, so many of us have made up our minds that fornication, adultery and even polygamy is okay.

Do you remember the lady at the well? Although she was not married to every man she had laid with, Jesus said they were her husbands. He was speaking from a biblical standpoint because sex is supposed to be saved for your spouse. You are physically wedding yourself without the spiritual yoking of God. With that being the case, you can't be mad at anyone except yourself when you find yourself dealing with an ugly custody battle.

Every one of Abraham's children was sent away, except for Isaac. Every one of them that had been sent away received a parting gift, but nothing was left to them in the will. Papa was a rolling stone. Wherever he laid his hat was his home, and when he died, all he left was a promise to Isaac.

Why We Have Religious Differences

After the rations Abraham gave them ran out, Hagar lost hope again. Like any good mother, she couldn't stand to watch her son die of starvation so, she left the child under a shrub and went off about fifty yards. She had forgotten her son's name was Ishmael, which in Hebrew means "God will Hear."

As Ishmael cried, God heard him, and "the angel of God called to Hagar from heaven and said to her, 'What is the matter, Hagar? Do not be afraid. God has heard the boy crying as he lies there. Lift the boy up and take him by the hand, for I will make him into a great nation.' Then God opened her eyes, and she saw a well of water. So, she went and filled the skin with water and gave the boy a drink" (Genesis 21:17-19).

God did as He promised. He was with Ishmael as he grew up. He lived in the desert and became an archer in the place called Mecca today. God also foretold that Ishmael would become a wild man who would dwell over and against all his kinsmen. He would be hated across the land, but he would be a mighty warrior and a strong nation. Ishmael had twelve sons, who became twelve tribes. His twelve sons settled primarily in the region to the east of the land that would become Israel. This fulfilled the promise God made to Hagar to make Ishmael and his offspring successful (Genesis 16:10–12). That was the birthing of the nation of Islam.

The split between the Islamic nation and the Christian nation comes from Jewish lineage. The Qur'an takes on the perspective of Ishmael, and the Bible takes a perspective of Isaac. Hagar's story is much more than the story of a concubine and her son. It is a story of God's care for those who have no hope. Our God is the same God who saw Hagar in her distress. Ours is the God who sees.

God Is Greater Than Our Past Mistakes

Although Abraham made the mistake of not trusting in God and waiting on the promise, God still honored His word and gave the promise to Isaac. We get so caught up in our own agony that we do not recognize that our victory is in God. The promise is our blood right as saved believers. It has nothing to do with what we can do ourselves on this earth, but it is about the rights we have as a child of God. God is more concerned about the relationship you and I have with Him than with rules and regulations.

Abraham was a model of faith and righteousness. His life was a faith journey, a sojourn to building a relationship with Christ. He had to believe he could bear a child with

Sarah at an old age. If he had not gone through this test, he would not have received the gift of the promised child. He had to pass the ultimate test of faith by submitting to God's command to sacrifice his long-awaited son, Isaac. Had he not gone through these tests that God had placed in his life, he would not have made it to where he was supposed to go. His willingness to sacrifice Isaac was a type and shadow of Jesus Christ. A type and shadow points us to future events. All of these steps contributed to Abraham becoming the man God intended him to be—Father Abraham.

Abraham's faith allowed Isaac to receive his birthright. Often, in the Body of Christ, we focus on generational curses. Rarely do we speak about generational blessings. Through Isaac, God granted a generational blessing of which you and I are still recipients even today. Any time you read in the Bible, "God of Abraham, Isaac and Jacob" you are dealing with the generational blessings we have as believers. We must stop spreading the notion of generational curses and focus more on generational blessings.

Illegitimate Child

One of the biggest generational curses we deal with today is women having children out of wedlock. I don't say women to be augmentative, but according to abortion laws, men have no say until birth. In reality, people having children out of wedlock is a large generational curse. Some of you who know me may say, "But pastor, you're not married. Don't you have a child?" I say, I must teach the Word of God, regardless of my past mistakes. I understand now that God is bigger than my past mistakes. I have to tell my truth also. It kills me every day that my daughter does not live with me. It kills me every day that I put myself in a situation I knew was wrong.

Living together out of wedlock, having sex outside of marriage, and receiving the news that I was having a child as the result of my sin, was a situation I could have prevented. I love my daughter, and she is the best thing in the world that has ever happened to me. One thing I know is that I can't wallow in self-pity. I must pick myself up and learn from my mistakes. I must have the certitude in God to cover my daughter in the world and carry on with my life.

I recognize that the pain I feel is common; many others in similar situations experience the same pain. If we allow God to use the pain, it will strengthen us. It draws us closer to God as we lean on Him and trust Him to do what He has promised in our lives. Isaac is not the only one to whom God has made a promise. God has chosen you to receive the promise of salvation through Jesus Christ. All you have to do is believe and receive. (Romans 10:9)

If you are reading this, you have probably heard or said the phrase, "I'm not laughing at you; I'm laughing with you." Most of the time, I believe I am not by myself. When I have said that to someone, I was, in fact, laughing at them. But I claimed to be laughing with them to lessen the sting of my laughing at them, and to make myself feel better. By saying I am laughing with them, it may appear to make it alright to laugh at the situation. However, that does not decrease or change the pain that the situation has brought in that person's life.

When I was in school, I struggled with reading. I didn't just struggle with reading in public, but I struggled with my personal reading as well. I would read a page in a book about seven or eight times before I could get an understanding of what the book was saying. Despite my difficulties with reading, God still got the last laugh. I have a career where I must read in front of people a minimum of once a week, if not every day.

When I was a child in the classroom, we did popcorn reading. Popcorn reading is when someone reads one paragraph, then calls on another individual to read the next paragraph. When I had to read in front of the class, I would stutter and misread words. Some of my classmates would poke fun and say I couldn't read. It felt like they would call on me to get a good laugh, and when I finished, I would call on another classmate, only to be called back on the next paragraph. I would find myself paying no attention to what the class was reading, but instead reading ahead so I could read clearly without being laughed at. I reasoned that when they laughed at me, they were really laughing at me.

I believe this is what happened with Hagar and Ishmael, and Sarah and Isaac. Hagar and Ishmael were saying they were laughing with them, but they were really laughing at them. They may have had a good laugh, but in reality, they had it wrong. Sarah remembered the promise, and she went to God. Her faith had grown a little faster than Abraham's. She finally understood that her son was the promised child. She believed that she had to protect her child's inheritance. She was not concerned about the promise to Ishmael. She realized she had messed up. She had waited 99 years for this, and she wasn't about to let Hagar take it away from her son. Sometimes you've got to fight like a lion but recognize that you are not always right. Sometimes you have to suck up your pride and tell your truth so that God can work the mess out in your life.

There is a saying called "digging in the dirt." Anytime God digs in the dirt, new life always follows. And because He's digging inside the dirty mess in your life, you must be candid enough to tell God, "I messed up, but I believe in the promise I received when I accepted Christ. I believe in the promise I received when I was baptized in the Name of Jesus, and I receive every bit of it."

If you're tired of hiding behind the perfect little image that you have convinced yourself you need to show everybody, this is the time to break free. You've got to talk to God and tell your truth. Many Christians beat themselves up about their past mistakes. Some have been taught that this somehow makes you holy. They ask for forgiveness, but it's just lip service because they are stuck in lies that contradict the truth of God's grace.

When we continue to condemn ourselves, we are saying, "Jesus, your blood could not possibly cleanse me." No matter what mistakes you've made in the past, first of all, know that you're in good company. Know that God uses our mess-ups when we fess up, step up, and accept His forgiveness. It's essential for us to receive His grace and move forward.

The best way to step into the freedom you received when you got saved is to confess the reality of your bondage and sin, and then repent. You must also repent for your unbelief.

In Abraham, we see that faith means trusting God's Word enough to risk living by it.

Brandon J. Addison

The Blessings of God

In 1542, Mary Queen of Scots took the throne of Scotland. Mary was raised Catholic, and Scotland was a Protestant country. Many of us who have been spoiled by the liberty of American democracy and freedom of religion may not see the concern here. During this time, monarchs would make decisions on how their people would worship, if allowed to worship at all. They understood what many miss in today's society—that this is all a holy war.

Mary, Queen of Scots, did something that was unthinkable during this time. After she was crowned Queen, she said that everyone could worship as they pleased. What's even more shocking is that when she was a widow to the King of France, a Catholic Scottish woman married an English Protestant nobleman, which gave her the right to the throne of England even though Queen Elizabeth I was on the throne at that time. This was something that had never been heard of before.

Queen Elizabeth was a barren woman. After the birth of Queen Mary's son James, Queen Elizabeth became his godmother and named him her successor to the throne of England. The King James Bible is named after Mary's son, James. He was the first king to sit on the throne of Scotland and England at the same time. He was also the first King to be Catholic and Protestant at the same time. King James took the Catholic Bible and translated it into a Protestant Bible in English so that his peasants in England and Scotland could read it.

Remember, the United States of America was founded on the belief that its people would have the freedom to worship as they please. America was constitutionally built on Christian morals, but as Christians, we ignorantly think that individuals will be saved by osmosis. Many Christians today believe that it takes no work on our part to bring others to salvation. They believe we only need to do what is right, show our light, and the rest of the country will fall into place and be saved too. We have watered down our belief so much that we just expect to see everyone on the other side of the Pearly Gates.

Then some people think because we've had president after president claiming to be Christian that all it takes to reach the American dream is to believe in God. However, that is treating God as if he were a magician or a genie in a bottle. We have come to believe that God is someone who can stand in the gap for us just long enough for us to enjoy our lives until we get old; then we decide it is time to slow down and begin to "live right." What this belief doesn't consider is that tomorrow is not promised to us.

After all of that, we have the audacity to treat individuals of Arabic descent as if they disgust us and have no right to be here. We do that as Christians. It's not just our race, but all different races treat them as if their lives are in danger whenever they are around us. We, as African Americans, should not treat them that way. We know how it feels to walk into a room full of people who do not look like us, and everyone turns around and stares. I refuse to pastor a church that would allow anyone to believe it is alright to treat people differently because they are of a different religion, race, or sexuality.

Christians should be able to sit down and have a conversation with people who differ from us and come to a better understanding of why they are the way they are. This is an enormous world, and we have to think more globally and spiritually regarding the people surrounding us. The more we understand the differences between people in our own backyard, the better we will understand people when God expands our territory.

This is the story of the birth of the Islamic nation. In the last chapter, we dealt with "What A Promise from God Looks Like." The promise of God may not come when you want it, but it will be there right on time. It is interesting how God will still fulfill His promise to you, even after you have failed Him. In this chapter, we are talking about the blessings of God. God blessed Abraham's son Ishmael even though Ishmael's birth was the result of Abraham, not trusting in God.

Twice God spoke to Hagar and told her to trust Him. He told her He would provide for her and her son. He told her she would not suffer the way she imagined, but she would suffer for a little while longer under Sarah. Then, He would make her son a *"Father of a great nation."* (Genesis 17:20)

Hagar found a wife for Ishmael. They bore twelve sons and one daughter, while living in the wilderness of Paran, which is said to be Mecca today, the home of the Islamic faith.

They journeyed through the wilderness until they finally came to a spot near some water. That is where they settled.

I don't know exactly how it worked—how a Hebrew man, Abraham, and an Egyptian woman, Hagar, created an Arabic son, Ishmael. Maybe when they mixed the bloodline of the Hebrews with the bloodline of the Egyptians, they got Arabic. Now if you talk to an Egyptian, they will tell you they have no Arabic lineage connection. They may even get offended and accuse you of degrading them. But if you take the DNA of an Egyptian person, you will find both Hebrew and Jewish lineage. But Arabic DNA shows a direct connection to Jewish lineage, just as claimed in the Quran. Don't take my word for it, but this is how I believe it happened.

The word "Islam" means peace through submission. An imam is like a pastor, the person who leads prayers in a mosque. I was listening to Imam Omar Suleiman, the founder and president of the Yaqeen Institute for Islamic Research in Dallas, Texas. He was in a remarkably interesting panel discussion with a rabbi and a pastor at Saint Michael and All Angels Church in Dallas, Texas.

He said that there are four brotherhoods in Islamic belief. Although they all read and memorize the same Quran, they have four different belief systems, or brotherhoods. Christians would call these a revelation or covenant. There are three different denominations within the Islamic belief system.

The first brotherhood is called the Adami, which means that they are the descendants of Adam. They believe we are all children of Adam, and they honor and identify as the children of Adam. Their belief is to treat everyone with respect regardless of who they are, what they look like or what they believe.

The second brotherhood is Brahami, which means they are descendants of Abraham. They believe we are all descendants of

Abraham, and the blessing comes from Abraham. Notice they believe the blessing comes from Abraham. We believe the promise comes through Abraham. There is a significant difference between the two.

The third brotherhood is called the Christ Muslims. They honor and recognize Jesus as the Christ. Just as there are Messianic Jews, there are Christ Muslims. These are the Muslims who have been changed by Jesus Christ. Now, this is where things get sticky. Jesus in Arabic is translated Isa. Jesus is mentioned 25 times in the Quran. In fact, after much investigation, I found that Jesus is mentioned more times in the Quran than Mohammad, who is only mentioned five times.

There are several revelations that come from that. One that we normally see is that some Muslims believe Jesus is a prophet. Although they are aware that He performed all the miracles listed in the Bible, and they even believe that Jesus, did, in fact, die on the cross for our sins, they still believe that He was just a prophet. When it comes to evangelism, if we can understand what other religions believe, it might make it easier to get them to hear and understand the Gospel.

The fourth and last brotherhood is the Brotherhood of the Mohammedi. They believe that the Prophet Mohammed is the direct descendant of Ishmael. They also believe he is the last in a long line of prophets that includes Moses and Jesus.

Muslims believe Muhammad was the chosen recipient and messenger of the Word of God through the divine revelations, which is how the holy Quran came about. His leadership is the founding of the 1400-year-old religion called Islam today.

I said all this to say that a simple conversation can help you come to understand the connection within the Abrahamic religions and to help you rightly divide what is true. Muslims view the Quran as the exact words of

God. Not divine truths given to the writer, but the actual words of God. They also respect the Hebrew Bible, the Oral Torah, and the Tanakh as holy and sacred Scriptures.

We know that as Blood-washed Believers we have been rebirthed into a generational promise of Abraham, Isaac, and Jacob. We are not blood right descendants, but we have been birthed into that promise. We are not of Jewish lineage, but we have been exalted by God based on the death, burial, and resurrection of Jesus Christ. Acts 28:28 tells us that Jesus came so that Gentiles could be saved too.

Remember, the entire Old Testament focuses on Jews and Gentiles and the separation between the two. You were either a Jew or a Gentile. There was nothing in between. But, once Jesus died on the Cross, whoever shall believe is no longer Jew nor Gentile, male nor female, slave or free, but all are children of God, knit together in eternity with the Father Almighty.

"But now that faith has come, we are no longer under a guardian, for in Christ Jesus you are all sons of God, through faith. For as many of you as were baptized into Christ have put on Christ. There is neither Jew nor Greek, there is neither slave nor free, there is no male and female, for you are all one in Christ Jesus."—Galatians 3:25-28 ESV

Let us take a look at what the Apostle Paul has to say. The Apostle Paul had written a letter to the Church of Galatia. Paul was a trained Pharisee under the well-respected Rabbi Gamaliel. Paul wrote the book of Galatians as a letter, as if he was a defense attorney in court defending his teachings of Jesus Christ to a panel of jurors in the person of the Church of Galatia.

"Tell me, you who want to be under the law, are you not aware of what the law says? For it is written that Abraham had two sons, one by the slave

woman and the other by the free woman. His son by the slave woman was born according to the flesh, but his son by the free woman was born as the result of a divine promise. These things are being taken figuratively: The women represent two covenants. One covenant is from Mount Sinai and bears children who are to be slaves: this is Hagar. Now Hagar stands for Mount Sinai in Arabia and corresponds to the present city of Jerusalem because she is in slavery with her children. But the Jerusalem that is above is free, and she is our mother. For it is written: "Be glad, barren woman, you who never bore a child; shout for joy and cry aloud, you who were never in labor; because more are the children of the desolate woman than of her who has a husband."

Now you, brothers, and sisters, like Isaac, are children of promise. At that time, the son born according to the flesh persecuted the son born by the power of the Spirit. It is the same now. But what does Scripture say? "Get rid of the slave woman and her son, for the slave woman's son will never share in the inheritance with the free woman's son." Therefore, brothers and sisters, we are not children of the slave woman, but of the free woman" —Galatians 4:21-31 NIV

Paul used Hagar and Sarah as examples of the flesh and the grace of God. We are all descendants of Adam. We are all made in the image and likeness of God. He blesses whoever He chooses. Favor ain't fair. He loves everyone on the earth as His child. Ishmael was one of Abraham's sons, so God blessed him. Although it stressed Abraham greatly to send his son away, God still blessed the mess Abraham created. But the promise was not in him. He did not receive the promise.

What is this promise of which I continue to speak? Great question! It is the promise of grace. What is the promise of grace? I am glad you asked. The promise of grace says that you are not judged, nor will you receive punishment for what you deserve. When Jesus died on the Cross, He activated the New Covenant, and we are now covered by grace.

I don't know about you, but I am so thankful that I am covered by grace. I am so thankful that I do not have to fight every day to believe I did everything right. I can wake up every morning and try my best to live according to God's way. I can wake up with confidence that if I do not wake up tomorrow, I will be at His feet, worshiping the King of Kings and Lord of Lords. I am confident that I will be lifting my praises saying Hosanna, Hosanna, Hosanna in the Highest! Hallelujah!

I praise Him that I no longer have to be a descendant of the flesh, even though I have made mistakes in the past. Although I cannot seem to get everything right, I know that through the grace of God, I, too, can be saved. I, too, can walk through those Pearly Gates. I, too, can have the victory. I, too, can receive the promise. I, too, can reach the victory in Jesus, and if He can do it for me, then, He can do it for you. The Promise of God is not just for me, we can both have the victory.

The most important part of what I want you to grasp is that we all must go from milk to meat. We want to get off breast milk and eat meat. (Hebrews 5:12-14) We want to rightly divide biblical truths, so we can go out and withstand the enemy with faithful confidence.

Every Bible character from Adam to Paul, with the exception of two, has died. Whether they went on home to be with the Lord, or whether they went to hell, they have gone on to their eternal resting place. Some people have chosen to have their bodies frozen with the belief that they can be thawed out and live forever. But not one of them has woken up—

only Jesus. So, no matter what anybody says, I am sticking with Jesus.

I am sticking with the Man who was born of a virgin, lived a life of perfection, was tortured, mocked, and spat on, was whipped until His flesh tore apart, was made to carry His Cross up a hill called Calvary, and was then put on display between a thief and a murderer like a common criminal.

I am sticking with the Man who hung on a cross with nails in His hands, nails in His feet, a crown of thorns on his head, pierced in His side, and yet He still prayed for me. If all that was not enough, He endured hell for me and suffered all the torture that I should have received. He shed His Blood as the sacrificial Lamb for the very last time. My God, my Grace, and my Lord, He has been so good to me.

I remember growing up attending Canaan Missionary Baptist Church in Louisville, KY, watching Dr. Walter Malone, Jr. Sometimes, he would not move a muscle in the pulpit. He was very cool, calm, and collected. Sometimes he would be in his office until it was time to preach. He would start his sermon nice and slow, then slowly unleash. Some weeks he would whoop, some weeks he would run. Some weeks he would walk pews. Other weeks he would teach a nice meaty sermon. The one thing that was always guaranteed was that before he would take his seat you would hear, "One day on a hill called Calvary, He died on that Cross, but after three days He rose from the dead." There was no way to get out of that service without him mentioning Jesus.

With everything going on in this world right now, the last thing we need is to fear death. We must remember that to be absent from the body is to be in the presence of the Lord. (2 Corinthians 5:6-8 KJV) There can be no resurrection without death. The purpose of our baptism is to be rebirthed into the resurrection of Christ, which washed away our sins that He bore for us on the Cross. (Acts 22:16) Those who are afraid to die don't believe that they are going to be resurrected. But when you know you are going to be resurrected, the rest of that doesn't matter because you are going to be in the presence of the Lord. There is no need to be fearful to be in His presence.

In Genesis, we find that an unhealthy type of sibling rivalry occurred between Isaac and Ishmael. It is the same type of rivalry that is tearing our churches apart today. We couldn't get it right back then because we couldn't decide and agree upon one thing, and we can't get it right today because we can't agree upon anything now. Churches are constantly split. Denominations are constantly being erected when we should just be the children of God.

Ishmael was sent away, but from the day that Isaac was born, he was with his father and learned the ways of his father. Ishmael only got half the story, and his descendants are still hurting. They are a mighty nation, but they don't proclaim Jesus Christ. They will not experience that glorious moment of walking into Heaven and holding hands with Christ. If you want to experience that moment, then you must believe on Jesus Christ for yourself.

Battlefield Of The Mind

The Grass may wither, the flowers may fade, but the word of God stands for ever God Thank you for your word. — Isaiah 40:8

"³⁹ Jesus went out as usual to the Mount of Olives, and his disciples followed him. 40 On reaching the place, he said to them, "Pray that you will not fall into temptation." 41 He withdrew about a stone's throw beyond them, knelt down and prayed, 42 "Father, if you are willing, take this cup from me; yet not my will, but yours be done." 43 An angel from heaven appeared to him and strengthened him. 44 And being in anguish, he prayed more earnestly, and his sweat was like drops of blood falling to

the ground. 45 When he rose from prayer and went back to the disciples, he found them asleep, exhausted from sorrow. 46 "Why are you sleeping?" he asked them. 'Get up and pray so that you will not fall into temptation." —
Luke 22:39-46

History began in a garden. Human history began in a garden. Human sin began in a garden and according to the last chapters of the Bible, humanity will end in a garden type city. It will appear to us as it comes towards us. In the Book of Revelations, we have a description that there will be a glassy sea, with the Tree of Life that will hang over everything in our new world (Revelation 4:6, Revelation 15:2).

Between those two gardens is a third garden, the Garden of Gethsemane, or the Mount of Olives. This is the garden where the true battle was fought, the battle that was fought for you and me. The battle being fought was for your salvation. I used to believe the battle was fought during the actions we choose, but I now realize that the battle was already won prior to the action we take.

Our mind is a battlefield, and there is an ongoing battle in our minds. Life began in the Garden of Eden, but new life began in the Garden of Gethsemane. When Adam sinned in the first garden, he lost life for himself and every person after him. In the second garden, Jesus, the second Adam, reclaimed the life Adam lost in the first garden. Adam ran and hid from God after he failed, but Jesus faced His battle head on, and prayed to the Father before His battle.

The Mount of Olives is a steep mountain that resembles a large rocky hill. At the base of the mountain is the Garden of Gethsemane. The Bible says in Luke 22:39, *"Jesus went out as usual to the Mount of Olives, and his disciples followed him."* What is interesting about that is the words, as usual. Have you ever had a place that you frequented? A place that you might always go to. For instance, maybe you prefer to use the same gas station to refuel your car, or maybe you frequent a particular restaurant. You do not need to look at the menu because you get the same thing every time you go. I'm talking about something that is familiar to you. The Mount of Olives was a place that Jesus loved. Perhaps He loved it because He could go to the top of the mountain and see the city of Jerusalem while He prayed.

Luke does not tell us the place where they are, but John 18 makes it very clear that there is a Garden of Gethsemane in the Mount Olives. Gethsemane in Hebrew is *gat shemanim*. *Gat* means the press, and *shamin* is the plural word for olives. This simply means that the Garden of Gethsemane is an olive oil factory, the place where olives are harvested. The oil from an olive is taken from the pit of the olive using an olive press. It's interesting that Jesus went to the olive press to experience his last pressing.

In the Bible days, olive oil had many uses, such as for food, for ointment, for illumination, and even for the manufacture of soap. Olives were very expensive. An olive is worth the most when it is crushed to make oil. T.D. Jakes wrote a wonderful book called Crushing. In his book, he used a great description of grapes being turned into wine.

Jakes said that a grape is an amazing fruit when it grows. You can take one and eat it, and it tastes sweet and juicy, but if you crush it, you get grape juice. Now what was used to nourish your body is now being used to hydrate your body, but if you let the grape juice ferment, it will turn into wine. The greatest state of a grape is wine. Once it has been crushed and fermented, it has been made new. This is the same concept with the olive.

Jesus was crushed right there in the Garden. Isaiah 53:5 says, *"But He was pierced for our transgressions; He was crushed for our iniquities; upon Him was the chastisement that brought us peace, and with His wounds, we are healed."* Jesus was crushed by the flesh's desire to find another way. We are all living through and dealing with a Garden of Gethsemane in our own lives. We all deal with some darkness, some struggles, and some temptations; a place where you are being crushed in your own life.

Luke 22:40 says, *"When He came to the place, He said to them, "Pray that you may not enter into temptation." He withdrew about a stone's throw beyond them, knelt down and prayed." (NKJV)* This was a normal practice for Jesus. He would always retreat and then go pray. Sometimes you need to find a place by yourself and then pray.

I love how specific Jesus is about telling them they need to pray. Jesus knew that their flesh could fall quickly into temptation, as He had previously prophesied. One disciple had turned Him in, and another denied Him three times. In fact, all His disciples claimed they would have no doubt in Him, but Thomas doubted Him after His resurrection. Jesus knelt on His knees in humbleness to pray.

I love the glimpse of the prayer we see in Luke 22:42, *"Father, if you are willing, take this cup from me; yet not my will, but yours be done."* (NIV) Then, an angel from Heaven appeared to Him and strengthened Him. Jesus, the Son of Man, humbled Himself enough to have an angel from Heaven come and strengthen Him. Jesus' prayer is a prayer I can see in many of our lives. If it's Your will, God take this cup from me.

The life of Jesus is recorded in all four Gospels. I truly believe anything put into this Bible four times must be of some importance. When reading all four Gospel accounts, you can put some perspective to the story. Jesus not only knelt on the ground, but He also lay prostrate to God. He had to get as low as He could to be strengthened from the angels. Jesus was above the angels, but He lowered himself beneath them in His flesh, in order to be strengthened by them.

The cup of sin for everyone in the world really hurts. Jesus knew what it would be like to die on the cross. He is the Alpha and the Omega, the Beginning, and the End, which means Jesus knew the anguish He would have to experience in hell for us. Luke 22:44 reads, *"And being in anguish, he prayed more earnestly, and His sweat was like drops of blood falling to the ground." (NIV)* Imagine what it would be like to take all humanity and put it on your shoulders. To have the entire world's fate in your hands.

We love to watch Marvel, DC, or sci-fi movies like The Day the Earth Stood Still, and we think it's cool to watch. Someone, usually a child or teenager, finds out they are the one with the missing key to save the world. I agree, they are great plots and very exciting in Hollywood. However, this is real life, in the real world. Jesus literally had to die on the Cross and experience the punishment for the sins of every person in the entire world.

Jesus experienced something called hematidrosis. Hematidrosis is a very rare condition in which humans sweat blood. It is caused from high-stress situations and the blood vessels in the sweat glands burst, causing your sweat to come out as blood. It is so rare that many people don't even know that it exists, but see, with Jesus, sweating blood has been seen throughout history. To those of you who believe your life is so stressful, if blood is not dripping from your pores, you are not stressing.

"When he rose from prayer and went back to the disciples, he found them asleep, exhausted from sorrow. "Why are you sleeping?" he asked them. "Get up and pray so that you will not fall into temptation."—Luke 22:45-46 NIV

I'm not mad at the disciples. I completely understand. When I first started taking my prayer life seriously, I would get up early to pray before I went to work, and I would always fall asleep. It was common for Jesus to be up early praying and starting the day, so it was likely that Jesus had them up very early. They had just eaten a meal, and just as so many of us do after we finish a meal, as soon as we sit down, we fall asleep.

In addition, the disciples had been very sad and discouraged with Jesus' persistence that His time had come, and His death was near. I can only imagine what it was like to walk next to Jesus in the flesh and then He claims He is leaving and will die. We already know the end of the story. Prophesy has been fulfilled.

With all that Jesus knew was coming, He urged them to stay focused. The same type of focus I urge you to have. We can't shrink away from our situation; we must push forward towards the mark. We must allow every situation and trial to motivate us to the next level in Christ.

All of this makes me think about Paul in his letter to the church of Corinth. Paul says in 2 Corinthians 12:8-10, *"Three times I pleaded with the LORD to take it away from me. But he said to me, "My grace is sufficient for you, for my power is made perfect in weakness."* Therefore, I will boast all the more gladly about my weaknesses, so that Christ's power may rest on me. That is why, for Christ's sake, I delight in weaknesses, in insults, in hardships, in persecutions, in difficulties. For when I am weak, then I am strong."

Paul is telling us we must see every situation in our life as something God is manifesting in our lives, positive or negative. Just because you are struggling with something, just because you are going through what you're going through, just because everything in your mind is telling you it's the last straw, just because you can't believe it, you have to keep trusting God.

Just because your life seems like it is out of control, and you feel like a deer caught in the headlights, and you don't know where to go next, you know where to go. Go to God. When your rent is due, light bill is due, water bill is due, and you still can't figure out how to feed the children, and to top it all off, it's Christmas, put it in God's hands. He knows what to do. Ask God to allow His power to rest on you.

Sometimes, you have to make hard choices in your life. Sometimes you have to decide about something that seems impossible, but day after day you keep on keeping on. You keep on trusting in the Lord. There may be that one thing that you can't seem to get past. I've tried my hardest to get rid of my one thing. Others say it's easy, but for me, I can't seem to get rid of it.

I'm not sure what your thing is, but I know you have one. We all have something inside of us we just can't seem to overcome. We have fought it tooth and nail, and nothing we do on our own can help us overcome. We gave our life to Christ, and that thing keeps creeping back up on us. We can't seem to find any refuge from it. We pray about it and pray about it. The Bible says Paul and Jesus, alike, prayed three times about it.

Do you realize that sometimes you are going through something in order for someone else to gain something from it? It might seem like hell in your life, and as much as you want to blame the devil for it, it just might not be him. Sometimes your sufferings come at the cost of someone else's rewards. It's not always a bad thing. As a pastor, I know that the suffering of pastorship comes at a great cost to our families, our mental health, and our physical health, but it is all worth it when you see lives being changed and souls being saved. You can pray all day, but some suffering is inevitable.

Paul asked God to remove the thorn from him, and God told him no. I know the feeling of anguish and the feeling that boils inside of you. Some suffering you create yourself. The self-control aspect of life holds a large part in our suffering. Some of the conditions in your life could have been prevented had you won the battle of your mind prior to the action you took. Your mind is a battlefield, and we have been given free will. With that free will, many people have taken the liberty to ignore the Spirit of God in their lives.

Paul prayed three times, but the thorn would not be taken from him. Jesus prayed three times and the cup would not be taken from Him either. Walking out of Gethsemane, Jesus knew His victory had already been won because He understood that He was facing the battle in His mind. No matter how strong He was, no matter how much God He was, He was still operating as a man. There were limitations, that's why it took an angel to strengthen Him.

I have learned it doesn't matter what your notion of who God is, but the Word of God says who He is. It doesn't matter how many degrees you have, how much power, or money you have, or what your race is, you are still just flesh. God gives and God taketh away. The flesh always has the possibility to go astray. No one is perfect.

I never realized how horrific my life was until I met the Lord—until I truly encountered Him. Through my walk with the Lord, I have come to realize that I have very little control over my flesh. The Holy Spirit's whole purpose is to teach us to control our flesh. There is a part of me that I just can't contain by myself. I would have felt bad for myself with this thorn in my side, just like Paul. I would have given up and thrown in the towel until I took a trip to Gethsemane and saw that Jesus struggled just like you and I struggle. It didn't matter how close He was to God He still came to a point where He struggled.

He had one job and that was to go to Calvary to save the world. When it came down to the time He was to die, He battled in His mind as He asked God to take the cup from Him. I have lost many battles in my mind before. I have even hidden the situation. The question is, can I defeat the battle in my mind before I move to the action and have to say I'm sorry later?

God does not disconnect my flesh. He leaves the flesh and puts His Spirit inside me. He allows the Spirit of God to guide my flesh and tell me what to do, where to do it, and how to do it. Just having the Word of God in me and the Spirit of God in me does not make my flesh say yes. There are times when I am battling in my mind about which actions to take. If I win the battle in my mind, then there are certain actions I won't take, but if I lose the battle in my mind, I am already on the way to the action I know I should not take.

Let me put it this way: You did not lose the battle when you got into that person's bed. You lost the battle when you picked up the phone. You knew you were married. You knew you were lonely. You knew that they knew just the right words to say to get you to come over. You knew your flaws, and you knew your issues. You thought about it all day. You battled with it in your mind all day, and when you picked up that phone, all you had to say was hello, and it was all over. You wrestled with it in your mind, so when you lost the battle in your mind, your body just rolled with the flow.

The battle of the mind is a battle each of us faces every single day, and every day we are to present our bodies as a living sacrifice, holy and acceptable to God. We are not to conform any longer to the world's way of thinking, but to be transformed by the renewal of our minds (Romans 12:1-2).

Philippians 4:8 tells us, *"Finally, brethren, whatsoever things are true, whatsoever things are honest, whatsoever things are just, whatsoever things are pure, whatsoever things are lovely, whatsoever things are of good report; if there be any virtue, and if there be any praise, think on these things."* We are told to take thoughts captive that are not so lovely, true, pure, or not of good report. We are to demolish arguments and every pretension that sets itself up against the knowledge of God, and we take captive every thought to make it obedient to Christ (2 Corinthians 10:5). It's much harder to take those thoughts captive once they gain momentum, so this is not something we should play around with.

Think about it. A fit and lean body doesn't just happen, neither does a healthy mind. Winning the battle of the mind takes intentional living and training. We must train our brain by intentionally thinking the kinds of thoughts outlined in Philippians 4:8. We must be persistent to guard our hearts, renew our minds, and shape our thought life with God's Truth.

No Resurrection Without Death

"²⁸ Do not be amazed at this, for a time is coming when all who are in their graves will hear his voice ²⁹ and come out-those who have done what is good will rise to live, and those who have done what is evil will rise to be condemned. ³⁰ By myself I can do nothing; I judge only as I hear, and my judgment is just, for I seek not to please myself but him who sent me."—John 5:28-30

Promise - Salvation

Most people do not take death well. In many cases, people have such a fear of what happens after death that they cannot bear to lose anyone. Have you ever heard the saying, "Ignorance is bliss?" But not in this case.

When you have the same hope that I have, you are able to deal with death differently. The spookiness of graveyards, the uncomfortableness of funeral homes, and the emptiness and sorrow that you feel on the inside when you are dealing with the passing of a loved one make dealing with death difficult. We, as a church, have done an injustice helping individuals understand what happens after death.

What absolutely blows my mind is the excitement we have over taking communion when it is the symbolic funeral of Jesus Christ. We remember the victory we receive over sin through the blood of Christ that is used to atone for us. We even lay the communion table at the altar and cover the body and blood with white cloths, just as Joseph and Nicodemus did inside of Jesus' borrowed tomb.

I did not get it until a few years ago when my cousin, Darren Ellis, died. My cousin went away for a few years, and when he got home just a few years later he died in a single car accident after sliding off the road. I thank God for the time I had with him and that I was able to help him get his life right with Christ. However, I mourned the time that I would no longer have to spend with him.

I prayed for my aunt and uncle as they went through the unthinkable task of burying their only son, and God led me to a scripture in 2nd Corinthians 5:8-10 that, in a nutshell, tells us that our time away from the body is in the presence of the Lord. When I read and understood that passage, my sorrow and mourning turned into an excited jealousy.

Now, I understand that jealousy is a sin, but that is not the kind of jealousy I am talking about. I'm talking about the type of jealousy the Bible tells us God has over our lives. The cousin I had that I loved so much is absent from the body and now in the presence of the Lord. I wished I could experience the greatness of Yahweh, the King of Kings and Lord of Lords, in person. The chance to lie at His throne and experience the paradise we call Heaven. I learned quickly growing up that I do not think like everyone else. They used to call me "the most" or "the dumbest around." Not because I was unintelligent, but because my way of thinking would throw people off quite a bit.

I started to put pieces of the puzzle together and started to get curious about the way death works. I understand the Bible tells me at the second coming of Christ, He will resurrect all, and we will go to your appointed place either Heaven or hell. When you die, you are in the presence of God, but you won't go until the second coming of Christ and the second resurrection. How do I come to grips with understanding that? Before I can go into the glory of what the resurrection means in our lives as Believers, I need to help you understand how cruel the sojourn to death was for Jesus.

According to 2 Corinthians 5:8, "We are confident, I say, and would prefer to be away from the body and at home with the Lord." And Hebrews 9:28 says, "so Christ was sacrificed once to take away the sins of many; and he will appear a second time, not to bear sin, but to bring salvation to those who are waiting for him." If read out of context, these verses seem like a contradiction straight out of the Bible.

Pope Benedict XVI used purgatory to help explain these two texts. He explains that there is a battle within you, a fiery battle that you must fight and work off your sins in the waiting period prior to entering the gates of heaven. I do not believe that is what the Bible says. That is not what I teach. If you had to work off all your sins, you would never make it to Heaven. The Mormons believe that you can be baptized for the dead if you do not believe they made it into Heaven. If that were the case, I would not be here right now. I would live my life however my flesh wanted, and I would pay someone to be baptized for me.

The best way for me to explain it is like this: go to Genesis 1:1, which says, *"In the beginning God created the heavens and the earth."* There is a lot of theology in this one verse, so let me unpack some of it for you. "Theo" means God, and "ology" means study of. So, let us break down this verse. It has an A and B clause. The A clause says in the beginning God. God in the Hebrew bible is written Elohim. El in Hebrew means "god." Ohim in Hebrew means "of Israel." Elohim together is a plural word meaning in the beginning was God the Father, Jesus, and the Holy Spirit.

Now, the B clause says, "created the heavens and the earth." Created being past tense. Heaven being plural and earth singular. God created all of this in the past tense before human creation. Heaven in the Hebrew translates to "sky." So, in Paul's letters, when he refers to his time on the Damascus Road, he talks about the third heaven. The first heaven is the tangible sky, where we see birds and clouds. The water cycle operates in the first heaven. The second heaven is our solar system. For example, the Milky Way is the area where the moon and stars reside. The Heaven of Heavens or the third heaven is where God resides. The word earth being singular disproves alien life form. He created the heavens... and the earth. Just because we see planets doesn't mean that there are life forms there.

In a nutshell, Genesis 1:1 is about creation. It is written so that anyone can understand it. That's how God operates. He's not trying to confuse you. But sometimes we forget that the Bible was not originally written in English, and we get confused once it's been translated. But when we break it back down to its original language, we get a better understanding of what the Bible is trying to say. 2 Peter 3:8 tells us that one day for God is like 1000 years to us. So, from that perspective, according to 2 Peter, it is as if God has experienced two days and 20 minutes since Jesus died on the Cross. I really want you to comprehend that.

Most people who lose a child do not move from the spot where they heard the tragic news of their child's death for more than two days because they remain in shock. They cannot sleep or eat because they are just thinking of all the things that they're going to miss with their child.

Think of the centuries of trials and struggles we have placed at God's feet within the first 48 hours of Him mourning His one and only Son. In Genesis 1:1, the A clause, "In the beginning God," tells us that God is and always has been. Prior to the concept of time or even the concept of heaven and earth, God existed. According to Genesis 1:1, God can operate in and out of time, but He is not limited by time.

The verses in 2 Peter used 1000 years: 1 day ratio to help give a diagram of how ridiculous it is for us to try and put a time stamp on

God's miraculous works. God is what we call omnipresent. An omnipresent God who operates in time but is not bound by time can literally resurrect every one of us at the same time, but at the different times of our deaths. You and I might die at a different time and immediately be in the presence of God, but we will be resurrected into the presence of God at the same time.

For example, if I were to die tonight, the next moment I would be home with the Lord. If you die next week, the next moment you will be with the Lord. Because of the omnipresence of God, we will arrive there at the same time at the Second Coming of Christ, the second resurrection also known as the Rapture. Huh? Revelation 21:4 says, *"And God shall wipe away all tears from their eyes; and there shall be no more death, neither sorrow, nor crying, neither shall there be any more pain: for the former things are passed away."*

You will not be in your own body, feeling and seeing the way we do here on this earth. You will be made new. The presence of everyone around you will be there, but you won't know who didn't make it there. There will be no need for drugs or alcohol. There is no need for sex because the experience of being in His face will overwhelm and overpower you. You will not be in mourning for those who did not make it, but in worship with God.

You may think this is morbid, but the truth is that Christ was born to die. The purpose of His existence was for Him to die. Without death, there is no resurrection. You see, everyone has an appointment with death. to die. It makes no difference what you do on this earth, you cannot extend your life, nor can you stop it short. It has all been predestined. Many of us struggle with the fact that tomorrow is not promised.

What Happens After Death

We all have an appointment to die. Hebrews 9:27 says, *"It is appointed for men to die once, but after this the judgement."* Most people live like they would never die, like tomorrow is promised. We have assembled ourselves in this world as if these things are what make us happy, content, and successful. The fact of the matter is, we all have an appointment to die, and we can't take anything that we have accumulated with us.

You cannot do anything to change the day you die or how you die. We think we are doing everything we can to help keep us alive, but perfectly healthy individuals can go to sleep and never wake up. People go into surgery for a simple procedure and never come out. They make caskets for all ages. You do not get multiple chances to die. There is no purgatory. There is no reincarnation.

A religious group called Sufism is a small Islamic group that will sacrifice themselves to receive a certain number of virgins in heaven.

There will be no sex in heaven. The biblical purpose of sex is to reproduce. With no reproduction necessary, there will be no sex, not even with your spouse. The Bible says there will be neither Jew nor Greek, slave nor free, male nor female, for you are all one in Christ Jesus.

There are three things that happen when you die. The first thing is that our bodies return to dust. Ecclesiastes 12:7 says, *"Then shall the dust return to the earth as it was: and the spirit shall return unto God who gave it."* The purpose for which we are buried in the ground is for our bodies to return to dust. My grandma and grandpa used to crack me up. My grandpa, George Addison, was a staunch Catholic. He believed everyone should be cremated. My grandma would always say, "That is great for him, but do not burn me up. Bury me like regular folks, just do not burn me up."

The second thing that will happen when we die is that our spirit returns to God, who gave it. Just as with your house mortgage, or your car loan, when the bank calls in your loan, everything must go back to them. Either the rest of the money, the house, or the car must be returned to the bank. God is the One who gave you life. God is your Creator, and when He calls you, you return to Him. That is why there is a yearning for you to be reconnected with your Father in Heaven.

It is human nature to believe in a higher power; to seek the reason for our existence. Every human being has a yearning to be reconnected to God. The key is whether you listen to it. Without Jesus Christ, you can never satisfy your yearning. You may try drugs, alcohol, sex, money, shopping, whatever, but none of that will satisfy the yearning for Christ. Only He can fill that void.

The third thing that happens to you when you die is that your soul goes to its eternal location, either heaven or hell. If you are saved, your soul goes to heaven, but if you are not saved, your soul goes to hell. 2 Corinthians 5:8 says, *"We are confident, I say, and willing rather to be absent from the body, and to be present with the Lord."* When a person dies who is a Christian, they will close their eyes here and open them on the other side. There is no time delay, it is an immediate response.

Let us look at what happens when a person who is not saved dies. In Luke 16:19-24 it says:

"There was a rich man who was dressed in purple and fine linen and lived in luxury every day. At his gate was laid a beggar named Lazarus, covered with sores and longing to eat what fell from the rich man's table. Even the dogs came and licked his sores. The time came when the beggar died, and the angels carried him to Abraham's side. The rich man also died and was buried. In Hades, where he was in torment, he looked up and saw Abraham far away,

with Lazarus by his side. So, he called to him, 'Father Abraham, have pity on me and send Lazarus to dip the tip of his finger in water and cool my tongue, because I am in agony in this fire.'"

Notice how prideful and boastful this rich man is. He is still trying to give orders from hell. He had part of his theology right, when he said "send Lazarus. Let him just dip the tip of his finger in water so I can quench my agony of hell." The rich man knew that just one drop of heavens water could cause all the fire in hell to burn out.

Verse 25-31 continues:

"But Abraham replied, 'Son, remember that in your lifetime you received your good things, while Lazarus received bad things, but now he is comforted here, and you are in agony. And besides all this, between us and you a great chasm has been set in place, so that those who

want to go from here to you cannot, nor can anyone cross over from there to us.'

"He answered, 'Then I beg you, father, send Lazarus to my family, for I have five brothers. Let him warn them, so that they will not also come to this place of torment.' "Abraham replied, 'They have Moses and the Prophets; let them listen to them.' "'No, Father Abraham,' he said, 'but if someone from the dead goes to them, they will repent.' "He said to him, 'If they do not listen to Moses and the Prophets, they will not be convinced even if someone rises from the dead." (ESV)

Listen to what that passage is saying. The rich man was asking for someone who was dead to go speak to his brothers, when they already had Moses and the prophets. What is so profound about this statement is that today we have Moses, the prophets, and Jesus and people still do not believe. I declare and decree that Jesus is alive and well. And if you just take a minute and accept Him into your life, you will come into a saving relationship with the Lord.

You do not have to live your life raggedy, boastful, and loose. However, if you feel like you want to live that way, then do whatever makes you happy. Because there will come a day that you will have to go before God and answer for everything you did in your life. You will have to answer for every decision you made, every action you took, every place you went, and the people you hung out with. You will have to answer to God. I don't know about you, but I am trying to do whatever it takes to hear my name read from of the Book of Life and hear the words, *"Well done my good and faithful servant! You can come on in." (Matthew 25:21)*

In some states, it is legal for physicians to assist people with suicide if the patient is terminally ill and will die within six months. The doctor can prescribe a pill that will help them die. There are a few things wrong with this. It is what we call humanism. Humanism is when we try to play the part of God. What if God had decided to heal that person? What if a child got his/her hands on the pills? Even worse, what if you got the medication for yourself and sprinkled it into the food of someone you do not like? I tell you this to encourage you to remember that God is the one who controls life. No matter how bad it gets, you must remember where your help comes from and allow Him to carry you through.

Now that we have some understanding of what death is and have an idea of what it will look like in heaven and in hell, let me remind you that Jesus endured the Cross, so we could be forgiven for our past, present, and future mistakes. Although Christ sits on the throne at the right hand of God Almighty, He still had to endure His time in hell for the sins that we committed.

What Christ Endured For Us

At 33 years of age, Jesus was sentenced to death by crucifixion, as recorded in Matthew 27:27-56, Mark 15:21-38, Luke 23:26-49, and John 19:16-37. Roman crucifixion was the worst type of capital punishment in those days, carefully crafted to make the person suffer an excruciatingly slow, humiliating, and painful death. Usually, only the worst criminals, slaves, and captive armies were sentenced to be crucified. Although He lived a sinless life, Jesus was nailed to the Cross by His hands and feet between two convicted criminals.

In the human body, there is a tendon in the wrist that extends to the shoulder. Most depictions of Jesus on the Cross have nails in the palm of His hands. However, Roman guards drove 6-8 inch nails through His wrists in this tendon, not in His palms as is commonly depicted. As the nails were being inserted into the wrist, the tendon would tear and break, forcing Jesus to use His ribs for support, so He could breathe.

His two feet were crossed together, and they hammered a larger nail through His arches, forcing Him to lean on the nail that tied His feet to the cross. Since Jesus could not support Himself with His legs because of the pain, it forced him to alternate arching His back. Then, to confirm that He was dead, a Roman guard pierced Him in His side with a spear. And the remaining blood and water in His body flowed from His wounds. Imagine the struggle, the pain, and the courage it took to endure such a horrible death. Jesus endured this for over three hours.

In preparation for the brutal crucifixion, they stripped Him of His clothing and put a scarlet robe on Him to mock Him as a fake king. They twisted together a crown of thorns and put it on His head. They put a reed in His right hand as a scepter to mock Him as the King of the Jews. They tied His hands to a post above His head and severely beat Him about His body and across His face with a flagrum, which is a whip made of several heavy, leather thongs knotted with bits of metal.

The lashes were so severe that chunks of flesh were torn off of His body and His face was ripped. After beating Him, the soldiers took the makeshift scepter and repeatedly struck Him across the head, driving the crown of thorns deep into His scalp. Most men would not have survived this torture. After this sadistic beating, they tied a heavy cross across Jesus' shoulders, and made Him walk almost two miles to the place of the crucifixion, while the crowd spat in His face and threw stones at Him.

Jesus had to endure this experience to open the Gates of Heaven, so that you and I can have access to God. So that our sins may be "washed" and carried away. All of them, without exception! Do not ignore the fact that Jesus Christ died for you!

The Truth About The Resurrection

John 5:28-29 says, *"Do not be amazed at this, for a time is coming when all who are in their graves will hear his voice and come out—those who have done what is good will rise to live, and those who have done what is evil will rise to be condemned." (NIV)*

Like Christ, everybody on this earth will be resurrected, but not everyone will go to Heaven. I am grateful that Jesus rose from the dead, because had He not, neither would we. And if you and I are not raised from the dead, we will never walk into the Throne Room of Grace.

The Apostle Paul said in 1 Corinthians 15:12-19, "But if it is preached that Christ has been raised from the dead, how can some of you say that there is no resurrection of the dead? If there is no resurrection of the dead, then not even Christ has been raised. And if Christ has not been raised, our preaching is useless and so is your faith. More than that, we are then found to be false witnesses about God, for we have testified about God that he raised Christ from the dead. But he did not raise him if in fact the dead are not raised. For if the dead are not raised, then Christ has not been raised either. And if Christ has not been raised, your faith is futile; you are still in your sins. Then those also who have fallen asleep in Christ are lost. If only for this life we have hope in Christ, we are of all people most to be pitied."

This passage tells us that if there is no resurrection of the dead, then Christ has not risen, and if Christ has not risen, then you and I are still in sin. Now, I can't speak for you, but I know I have walked out of my sins. I know I have passed from death to life. I know there has been a change in my life, and if the change in my life is proof that Jesus has risen, then I know He has risen.

Something has transformed in my life. I know I am not the same person I used to be. I do not act the way I used to act. I don't think the way I used to think. I don't talk the way I used to talk. I don't live the way I used to. When I just think about the breath in my body, the life still in me, I want to give Jesus an undignified praise. However, when I think about Him on that cross, I cannot help but lose control. He has changed me. Has something changed in you? Has your life been transformed?

Brandon J. Addison

Straightway

The Gospel according to Mark is one of the first accounts of the life of Jesus. It was written by a Christian scribe named Mark, or John Mark. Mark was not one of Jesus' twelve disciples, but he was incredibly involved with the early Christian church. In fact, his mother, Mary, hosted the first Christian church in her home. He was a co-worker with Paul and a close friend of Peter. This account of the Gospel was written primarily from his work with Peter, Luke, Paul, and Barnabas. In this chapter, we will examine the death, burial, and resurrection of Christ, through His baptism.

The Old Testament ends with the Book of Malachi. There are 400 years of silence from God. Nobody had spoken to Him or His angels until in the first chapter of Luke, but then the angel Gabriel appeared to Zechariah as he was serving in the temple. When Zechariah saw him, he was frightened.

"But the angel said to him: "Do not be afraid, Zechariah; your prayer has been heard. Your wife Elizabeth will bear you a son, and you are to call him John. He will be a joy and delight to you, and many will rejoice because of his birth, for he will be great in the sight of the Lord. He is never to take wine or other fermented drink, and he will be filled with the Holy Spirit even before he is born. He will bring back many of the people of Israel to the Lord their God. And he will go on before the Lord, in the spirit and power of Elijah, to turn the hearts of the parents to their children and the disobedient to the wisdom of the righteous—to make ready a people prepared for the Lord.

Zechariah asked the angel, "How can I be sure of this? I am an old man, and my wife is well along in years." The angel said to him, "I am Gabriel. I stand in the presence of God, and I have been sent to speak to you and to tell you this good news. And now you will be silent and not able to speak until the day this happens, because you did not believe my words, which will come true at their appointed time." —Luke 1:13-20 NIV

Elizabeth did indeed become pregnant, just as the angel said. When she was in her sixth month, the angel Gabriel appeared to her relative Mary, proclaiming that she would conceive a child by miraculous conception. He told her that her relative Elizabeth, who was barren, was six months pregnant with a son in her old age, for with God, nothing is impossible. Mary traveled to her relative's house and spent three months with her.

Upon arrival, with just one word from Mary, the unborn child in Elizabeth's womb leaped in her womb. Even from Elizabeth's womb, the unborn child recognized the presence of God in Mary's womb. Elizabeth was filled with the Holy Spirit and began to prophesy to Mary. This was fulfilling the promise that was given to Zechariah that his son would move in the spirit of Elijah (Luke 1:16-17).

After the birth of the child, per Jewish custom, on the eighth day, Zechariah and Elizabeth took their son to be circumcised. Friends and family urged them for a name, and they said, "John." It was a name that shocked everyone because it had no family lineage. Zechariah was from the family of Levi, which holds the priesthood. Naming a child needed to be in the lineage of the priesthood. Immediately after Zechariah wrote in the family records the name John, Zechariah was able to speak again and began praising God (Luke 1:64).

In Mark 1:1, He makes the only personal opinion in his entire book when he says, *"the beginning of the good news about Jesus the Messiah, the Son of God."* Through the rest of the Book, he allows the facts of Jesus' work to speak for itself. Verses 2-3 make it clear that the birth of John is the fulfilment of Isaiah's prophecy,

"A voice cries: "In the wilderness prepare the way of the Lord; make straight in the desert a highway for our God." (Isaiah 40:3)

John became known as John the Baptist because he was out in the wilderness crying, *"Repent, repent, repent!"* and baptizing people. In the beginning, people didn't want to listen to John the Baptist. But something happened, and the Scripture says Jerusalem and all Judea and all the region about the Jordan were going out to him, and they were baptized by him in the river Jordan, confessing their sins.

What is even more interesting is when the angel visited Zechariah prophesying the birth of his son, he was told by the angel that his son would come forth and operate under the power of Elijah. Elijah performed many miracles, but John did not perform any, except bringing the masses in to confess their sins and be baptized. John the Baptist spoke of One who would come whose sandals he was not worthy to loosen. He knew that the glory of the One who was still to come was much greater than yours or mine. These revelations elevated Jesus and humbled John the Baptist.

Teachers in the Jewish culture could ask anyone of their students to do anything besides take off their shoes. It was beneath them to ever ask someone to loosen their sandals. It was acceptable to offer to remove someone else's shoes and wash their feet out of respect for who they were, but it was blatant disrespect and never acceptable to ask someone to remove your shoes from your own feet. John was saying that Jesus was so holy that he (John) was too lowly to even touch Jesus' shoes, let alone take them off.

That is why he spent time contrasting his ministry to Jesus'. He said, "I baptize you with water, but the One to come baptizes you with the Holy Spirit." Here in lies the denominational argument. Should one baptize in Jesus' Name or in the Name of the Father, the Son, and the Holy Spirit? John the Baptist is saying that he can only give you a symbolic baptism of the inward move of God in your life.

In other words, John the Baptist can baptize you all day with water, but it means nothing if you do not confess your sins and repent. To repent means to turn away from your sins. Recognize that Jesus is King and His salvation through death on the Cross saved us from all our sins.

Mark 1:9 says, *"At that time Jesus came from Nazareth in Galilee and was baptized by John in the Jordan."* In the gospel account of Matthew, we learn that when Jesus arrived John did not want to baptize Him because John didn't count himself worthy. He proclaimed that Jesus should be baptizing him. Jesus told him he had to show the world what they needed to do. He had to show the representation of His death in order to be resurrected.

The Greek word for baptize is "baptize" which means to immerse or to submerge. This is why I believe in a full submerging baptism. How do you bury someone by sprinkling? Mark 1:10-11 talking about Jesus says, *"And straightway coming up out of the water, he saw the heavens opened, and the Spirit like a dove descending upon him: And there came a voice from heaven, saying, Thou art my beloved Son, in whom I am well pleased."*

I said earlier that everyone has an appointment to die, and everyone will be resurrected. The baptism represents Christ's death, burial, and resurrection. It is a symbolic rebirth into the family of God. For example, when you are dead, you lay down in your coffin and are placed into your grave. But when you are resurrected, you will rise again brand new. When you are baptized you will rise again brand new. That is the symbolic purpose of the submerging. When I was baptized, I literally felt lighter, like I shed weight coming out of the water. I felt like I left all my burdens at the altar, and I could start off fresh anew.

Notice where it says "straightway." Webster defines straightway as "extending or moving in a straight line." The Greek translation for "straightway" is euthus (pronounced yoo-thoos') meaning "directly at once, immediately, forthwith." In other words, as soon as Jesus' nose broke the surface of the water, the Spirit of the Lord came down upon him like a dove.

That reminds me of Genesis 28:12-13 which says, "He had a dream in which he saw a stairway resting on the earth, with its top reaching to heaven, and the angels of God were ascending and descending on it. There above it stood the Lord, and he said: "I am the Lord, the God of your father Abraham and the God of Isaac. I will give you and your descendants the land on which you are lying."

Jacob, tired from traveling, placed his head on a rock to go to sleep. When you see a rock in the Old Testament it refers to Jesus. Jacob saw a ladder with angels ascending and descending on it. Jacob said to himself, "I need to mark this place so I know where I can have access to God."

It is human nature for us to yearn to be back in the presence of the Lord. When you come into a saving relationship with Christ and are baptized through His death, burial, and resurrection, your ladder to Heaven follows you. The Bible says straightway the heavens open, and the Spirit of God descends upon you. Once washed clean by Jesus' blood, you have continual access to the open the windows of Heaven. The Bible says, as Jesus died, the veil of the temple was torn in two from top to bottom. The veil was a heavy curtain that separated the second room called the Holy of Holies from the first room, the Holy Place.

How do we know the heavens are still open above us today? "But Stephen, full of the Holy Spirit, looked up to heaven and saw the glory of God, and Jesus standing at the right hand of God. "Look," he said, "I see heaven open and the Son of Man standing at the right hand of God." (Acts 7:55-56)

In this passage, Stephen is being stoned to death for preaching about the Messiah Jesus. The Bible says, he looked up and saw the glory of God. He said he saw Jesus standing at the right hand of God. Up until now in the Bible, Jesus sits at the right hand of God. The Bible doesn't say why Jesus stood in Stephen's vision, but when we see royalty standing in the Bible it is either out of anger or out of respect (Jonah 3:4-10, 2 Kings 23:1-3). I believe Jesus was honoring Stephen and giving him a standing ovation.

Do you want a standing ovation from God? Do you want to hear God say you are My child, and I am greatly pleased? Just as our Jesus stood to honor Stephen at his death, so He will do for all of His children who faithfully serve Him.

"Therefore, my dear brothers and sisters, stand firm. Let nothing move you. Always give yourselves fully to the

work of the Lord because you know that your labor in the Lord is not in vain"—1 Corinthians 15:58

About The Author

Rev. Brandon J. Addison majored in religion at Simmons College of Kentucky. Rev. Addison March 2018 and was licensed at Lindsey Wilson College in May 2019. He was appointed by the United Methodist church as the associate pastor of amazing grace community of faith UMC in July 2019.

Pastor Addison was called to plant The Kingdom Advancement Cathedral of worship July 5th, 2020. Soon after taking over as CEO of God's Grill, CDC. Pastor Addison founded Addison Ministries and is now known around the country as the originator of the HopeBoyz movement. (No longer serving dope now we're serving hope.) Rev. Addison is humbled and honored to be called to teach and preach the gospel of Jesus Christ.